READING SUCCESS FOR

MINECRAFTERS

Grades 1-2

Illustrated by Amanda Brack

Sky Pony Press
New York

Sky Pony Press books may be purchased in bulk at special discounts for sales promotion, corporate gifts, fund-raising, or educational purposes. Special editions can also be created to specifications. For details, contact the Special Sales Department, Sky Pony Press, 307 West 36th Street, 11th Floor, New York, NY 10018 or info@skyhorsepublishing.com.

Sky Pony® is a registered trademark of Skyhorse Publishing, Inc.®, a Delaware corporation.

Visit our website at www.skyponypress.com.

10 9 8 7 6

Library of Congress Cataloging-in-Publication Data is available on file.

Cover design by Brian Peterson

Cover illustration by Amanda Brack

Book design by Kevin Baier

Print ISBN: 978-1-5107-3088-5

Printed in the United States of America

A NOTE TO PARENTS

When you want to reinforce classroom skills at home, it's crucial to have kid-friendly learning materials. This *Reading Success for Minecrafters* workbook transforms reading practice into an irresistible adventure complete with diamond swords, zombies, skeletons, and creepers. That means less arguing over homework and more fun overall.

Reading Success for Minecrafters is also fully aligned with National Common Core Standards for 1st and 2nd grade English Language Arts (ELA). What does that mean, exactly? All of the reading exercises in this book correspond to what your child is expected to learn in school. This eliminates confusion and builds confidence for greater homework-time success!

As the workbook progresses, the reading becomes more advanced. Encourage your child to progress at his or her own pace. Learning is best when students are challenged, but not frustrated. What's most important is that your Minecrafter is engaged in his or her own learning.

Whether it's the joy of seeing their favorite game characters on every page or the thrill of discovering new words, there is something in this workbook to entice even the most reluctant reader.

Happy adventuring!

SHORT A

*Draw a line to connect the picture with the **short a** word.*

apple

map

bat

axe

cat

SHORT A

*Finish each sentence with one of these **short a** words.*

apple   map   bat   axe   cat

1. I eat a golden _____ so I can get hunger points.

2. The _____ flies around the cave.

3. The _____ helps me find my way around.

4. My black _____ likes to eat fish.

5. I chop down trees with my _____.

LONG A

*Draw a line to connect the picture with the **long a** word.*

cake

play

blaze

lay

race

LONG A

*Finish each sentence with one of these **long a** words.*

cake   **play**   **blaze**   **lay**   **race**

1. Steve made a _____ for Alex's birthday.

2. She is attacked by the yellow _____ .

3. Steve will _____ back to safety.

4. The chicken will _____ five eggs.

5. Steve likes to _____ and have fun.

SHORT E

*Draw a line to connect the picture with the **short e** word.*

Enderman

skeleton

egg

bed

red

SHORT E

*Finish each sentence with one of these **short e** words.*

Enderman   skeleton   egg   bed   red

1. The purple _____ has a shulker inside.

2. The block is _____ .

3. Steve will battle the bony _____ .

4. You can build a _____ with wood.

5. The tall, black _____ is afraid of water.

LONG E

*Draw a line to connect the picture with the **long e** word.*

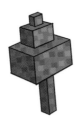

beef

creeper

tree

wheat

she

LONG E

*Finish each sentence with one of these **long e** words.*

beef   creeper   tree   wheat   she

1. Steve feeds bunches of _____ to the horse.

2. Destroy a cow and you can collect raw _____ .

3. Don't get too close to a _____ when
    it explodes.

4. Plant saplings if you want a _____ to grow.

5. Alex wears her armor when _____ wants to win a battle.

SHORT I

*Draw a line to connect the picture with the **short i** word.*

fish

pickaxe

squid

Wither

pigman

SHORT I

*Finish each sentence with one of these **short i** words.*

fish   **pickaxe**   **squid**   **Wither**   **pigman**

1. A zombie _____ spawns when lightning strikes near a pig.

2. A diamond _____ is a very good tool for mining.

3. The black _____ swims in the water and drops ink.

4. The _____ has three heads!

5. When I get hungry, I can try to catch a _____ .

LONG I

*Draw a line to connect the picture with the **long i** word.*

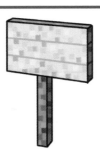

ice block

iron golem

night

ride

sign

LONG I

*Finish each sentence with one of these **long i** words.*

ice blocks   iron golem   night   ride   sign

1. You can break _____ in the Artic biome.

2. The _____ is a neutral mob that protects villages.

3. You can write what you want on the wooden _____ .

4. Zombies and other scary mobs come out at _____ .

5. Jump in and _____ in a minecart!

SHORT O

*Draw a line to connect the picture with the **short o** word.*

cobweb

ocelot

block

zombie

donkey

SHORT O

*Finish each sentence with one of these **short o** words.*

cobwebs   ocelot   blocks   zombie   donkey

1. I feed the _____ some fish to tame it.

2. I build a shelter with ten granite _____ .

3. The moaning _____ only attacks at night.

4. There are _____ hanging in the spider's cave.

5. A _____ looks a lot like a horse.

grow

bone

arrow

potion

explosive

LONG O

*Finish each sentence with one of these **long o** words.*

grow   bone   potion   arrow   explosive

1. The flower will _____ in the garden.

2. Feed the wolf a _____ and it will be your pet.

3. Use a _____ of Swiftness to escape the creeper.

4. The skeleton shoots an _____ at Steve.

5. Blocks of TNT are great for setting _____

   traps.

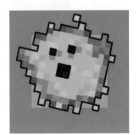

SHORT U

*Draw a line to connect the picture with the **short u** word.*

 **pufferfish**

 mushroom

 **hunger bar**

 **bucket**

 bunny

SHORT U

*Finish each sentence with one of these **short u** words.*

| mushrooms | pufferfish | hunger bar | bucket | bunny |

1. The white _____ hops over to Steve.

2. A _____ full of water can scare Endermen away.

3. The bony _____ tells a player if they

need to eat.

4. I catch a _____ with my fishing rod.

5. Alex picks the red _____ to make stew.

LONG U

*Draw a line to connect the picture with the **long u** word.*

huge

blue

cube

fruit

suit

LONG U

*Finish each sentence with one of these **long u** words.*

blue   huge   cube   fruit   suit

1. The color of the bucket is _____ .

2. Each block in the game is shaped like a _____ .

3. Alex puts on a _____ of armor to battle the Ender Dragon.

4. An apple is a kind of _____ .

5. The giant zombie looks _____ next to the villager.

SENTENCES

*A **sentence** is a group of words that tells a complete thought. All sentences begin with a **capital letter**. A statement ends with a **period**. A sentence includes a **noun**, a **verb**, and sometimes an **adjective**.*

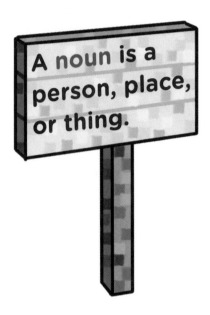

A noun is a person, place, or thing.

A verb is an action word.

An adjective is a description word.

1. *Draw a triangle around the **capital letter** that begins the sentence.*

2. *Circle the **noun** (there may be more than one).*

3. *Underline the **verb**.*

4. *Draw a rectangle around the **adjective**.*

5. *Draw a square around the **period** that ends the sentence.*

1. The green creepers dance.

2. The player crafts an iron sword.

3. Alex fills the open chest.

4. The baby zombie rides a chicken.

5. The skeleton shoots a sharp arrow.

THE PIG

*Read about the Minecraft pig.
Then write **true** or **false** for the statements on the
next page.*

This is a pig. Pigs spawn on grass blocks.

Pigs roam the Overworld. They do not like

water. Baby pigs are called piglets. Piglets

grow into pigs in twenty minutes.

1. Pigs spawn on sandstone. _____

2. Pigs live in the Overworld. _____

3. Pigs like water. _____

4. A piglet is an adult pig. _____

5. It takes twenty minutes
   for piglets to grow into pigs. _____

THIS IS THE WOLF

Read about the wolf.
Then connect the phrases in the left column with the correct answers in the right column.

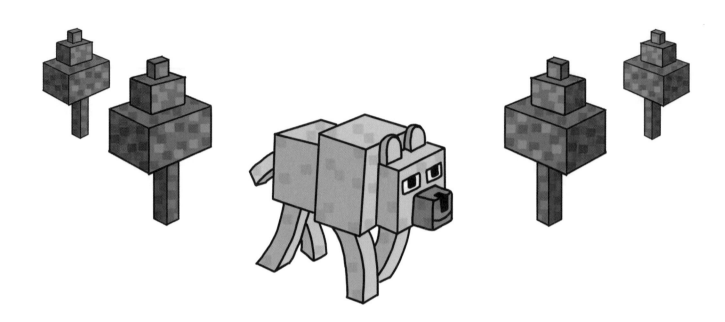

This is a wolf. The wolf has gray fur. He can be wild, mean, or tame. A wild wolf has black eyes. A mean wolf has red eyes. A tame wolf has a red collar. The wolf lives in a pack. Wolves spawn in packs of four.

The wolf's fur is ...

black eyes

A wild wolf has ....

a red collar

A mean wolf has ....

gray

A tame wolf has ....

red eyes

MEET THE COW

Read about the cow.
Then answer the questions on the next page.

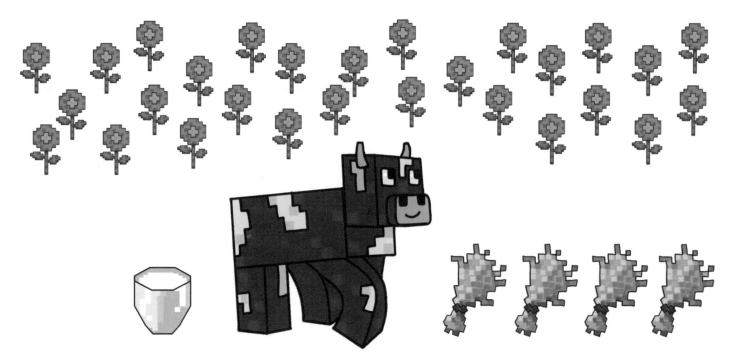

This is a cow. The cow has gray spots.

Cows walk slowly. Cows will follow wheat.

If you have a bucket, you can milk a cow.

1. What color are the cow's spots?

The cow's spots are _____ .

2. How do cows walk?

Cows walk _____ .

3. What does a cow follow?

A cow follows _____ .

4. What do you need to milk a cow?

You need a _____ to milk a cow.

SADDLE UP!

Read about the horse.
Then use the words to fill in the blanks on the next page.

Horses come in seven colors. Some horses

have spots. This horse is eating carrots.

He likes carrots because they are crunchy.

A saddle lets you ride the horse. It takes

a long time to tame a horse. The horse is

tame when it shows hearts. Some horses

can jump high.

Choose from the words below to fill in the blanks.

black	tasty	crunchy
brown	seven	farms
flowers	saddle	hearts

1. The horse comes in _____ colors.

2. The horse likes eating carrots because they are _____ _____ .

3. A _____ lets you ride the horse.

4. When a horse is tame, it shows _____ .

WATCH OUT FOR ZOMBIES!

Read about zombies. Then answer the questions on the next page.

This is a zombie. Zombies are slow, so it is easy to run away from them. Their groaning sounds let you know they are nearby. Sunlight can kill a zombie.

Zombies can call other zombies to help them fight. If a zombie attacks you, it can turn you into a zombie too.

1. Zombies are

   ☐ Fast   ☐ Slow   ☐ Quiet

2. What kind of sounds do zombies make?

   ☐ Moaning   ☐ Screaming   ☐ Groaning

3. What can kill a zombie?

   ☐ Sunlight   ☐ Darkness   ☐ Other zombies

4. Who can zombies call to help them fight?

   ☐ Wolves   ☐ Other zombies   ☐ Dragons

5. If a zombie attacks you, it can turn you into a

   ☐ Robot   ☐ Zombie   ☐ Zombie robot

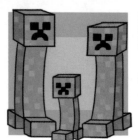

CREEPY CREEPERS

Read about creepers.
Then finish the statements on the next page.

Creepers are green and very quiet. They

like to hide in caves. Creepers will sneak

up on you and then explode. This will

harm anything near the blast. They are

afraid of cats, so keep a cat with you at

all times. Climbing a ladder to escape a

creeper will not work. It's better to hide

behind closed doors.

1. Creepers can sneak up on you because they are

_____

- - - - - - - - - - - - - - - - - - -

_____ .

2. Creepers might be hiding in a

- - - - - - - - - - - - - - - - - - - -

_____ .

3. If they

_____

- - - - - - - - - - - - - - - - - -

_____ , you could be harmed.

4. Creepers have a fear of

- - - - - - - - - - - - - - - - - -

_____ .

5. Creepers can't open doors, but they can climb

_____

- - - - - - - - - - - - - - - - - -

_____ .

THE ENDER DRAGON

Read about the Ender Dragon.
Then fill in the blanks on the next page.

The Ender Dragon is a boss mob. It lives in the End. It flies in circles in the sky. It can charge at players. It likes to perch on the tallest block. It can send out purple balls of fire. Some Ender Dragons drop an egg when destroyed.

1. The Ender Dragon is a _____ mob.

2. The dragon lives in the _____.

3. The dragon flies in _____ in the sky.

4. The balls of fire are _____.

5. To get an egg from an Ender Dragon, you have to

_____ it.

MINECRAFT BOATS, NEW AND IMPROVED

Read about Minecrafters' boats.
Then answer the questions on the next page.

The boats in the new version of the game are much better than the boats in the old version. The new boats are stronger and don't break apart so easily. They also come with paddles. The boats in the new version go faster than the boats in the old version. Plus, the new boats can carry two people. They are a new great way to move around.

What is the main idea of this text?

_____

- -

_____

- -

_____

Give three details that support the main idea.

_____

1. -

_____

_____

2. -

_____

_____

3. -

_____

THE GHAST

Read about ghasts.
Then circle the correct answer to the questions on the next page.

The ghast was floating in the Nether world. Its eyes and mouth were closed. Its legs swayed gently. The ghast was sad because it could not leave the Nether world. Then it sensed someone was nearby. It opened its black mouth and eyes. It made high-pitched screams. The ghast shot its fireballs at the enemy, who hid behind a wall. The ghast floated and dropped more fireballs. An arrow flew by its legs. Then more arrows flew by even closer. The fight was on!

1. The ghast:

   A. Moved quickly   B. Floated   C. Stayed in one place

2. The ghast was:

   A. Happy   B. Excited   C. Sad

3. The ghast's mouth and eyes are:

   A. White   B. Black   C. Red

4. The ghast shot:

   A. Fireballs   B. Arrows   C. Screams

5. The arrow almost hit the ghast's:

   A. Head   B. Mouth   C. Legs

ALL ABOUT POTIONS

Read about potions.
Then fill out the chart on the next page.

Potions give you special powers. To make potions, you must get certain things from the Nether. You also need to have a brewing stand. Almost all potions start with a base potion. Some potions are green, blue, purple, red, yellow, or orange. A green potion lets you jump high. A blue potion lets you see at night. A purple potion brings you back to health. A red potion makes you stronger. A yellow potion gives you a health boost. An orange potion protects you from fire.

Potion Colors and Their Effects

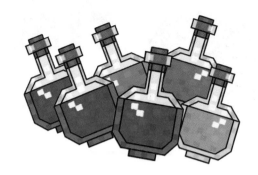

COLOR	EFFECT
Green	
Blue	
Purple	
Red	
Yellow	
Orange	

STEVE'S BIRTHDAY

Read the story about Steve's birthday.
Then answer the questions on the next page.

Today is Steve's birthday, and he turns nine. He is very excited to have a party. He hopes he gets a new video game for a present. His friends will come over at four o'clock for cake and ice cream. But the cake looks so good. Steve thinks it will be okay if he just tries a small piece. Yum! It is so tasty! Steve thinks he will take another slice. He can smooth the frosting over what he has eaten and no one will notice. The frosting is so good, too! Maybe just another little piece. Uh oh! The cake is almost gone now. Steve hears his mom in the hall.

"Steve!" she yells. "You ate all the cake! I told you to leave the cake alone. You will have to call your friends and tell them the party is cancelled!"

1. What is the cause of the mother's anger?

_____

_____

_____

_____

_____

_____

_____

2. What is the effect of the mother's anger?

_____

_____

_____

_____

_____

_____

_____

SKELETONS AND ZOMBIES

Read about skeletons and zombies.
Then use the facts and the Venn diagram to
compare and contrast their traits.

Skeletons like to travel in mobs. They will burn in sunlight and try to stay in the shade as much as they can. However, a skeleton will be protected if it is wearing a helmet. Skeletons drop bones and arrows. They cannot see through glass. Skeletons are hard to defeat.

Zombies are often found in mobs. Sunlight can kill a zombie but a helmet will protect it. Zombies drop rotten flesh, carrots, and potatoes. Zombies are very slow, so it is easy to defeat them. Zombies are unable to see through glass.

FACTS

SKELETONS

Travel in mobs

Are burned by sunlight

Hard to defeat

Drop bones and arrows

Are protected by helmets

ZOMBIES

Travel in mobs

Are burned by sunlight

Easy to defeat

Drop rotten flesh, carrots, and potatoes

Are protected by helmets

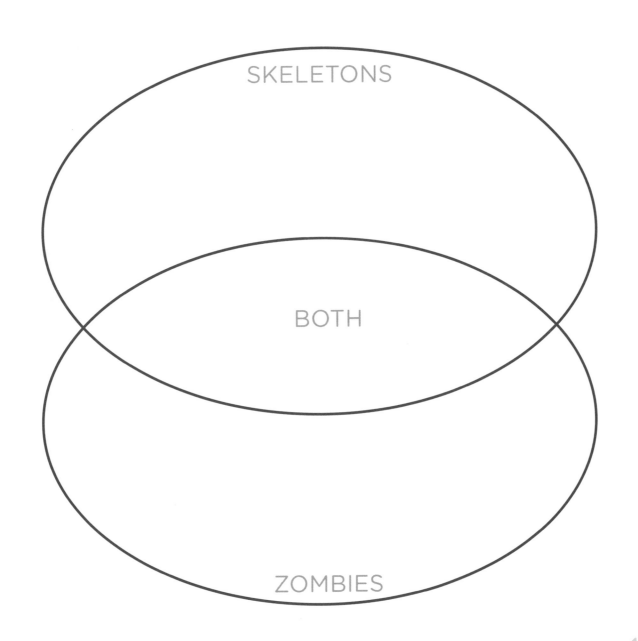

SKELETONS

BOTH

ZOMBIES

STEVE'S GARDEN

Read about Steve's garden.
Then number the events in the story in the order in which they happened.

Steve will need food. The best way to get food is to grow a garden. First Steve needs to make a hoe. Then he clears a flat spot for his garden. He collects seeds. Next, he tills the soil with his hoe and plants the seeds. Then he digs a hole in the ground for water. He pours water into the hole with a bucket. The garden needs lots of light. He puts a torch next to his crops. The torch will also keep monsters away.

_____ Steve clears a flat spot for his garden.

_____ Steve collects seeds.

_____ Steve digs a hole for water.

_____ Steve makes a hoe.

_____ Steve puts a torch next to his crops.

_____ Steve plants the seeds.

ALEX AND HER DIAMOND ARMOR

Read the story about Alex.
Then fill out the chart on the next page.

Alex is wearing her diamond armor. It is the strongest armor of all. Alex needed 24 diamonds to make her set of armor. She needed 5 diamonds to make her helmet. She needed 8 diamonds to make her chestplate. To make leggings she needed 7 diamonds. Her boots were made with 4 diamonds. With her diamond armor and sword, Alex can do anything! She might save a village or destroy a mob. Watch out!

Diamonds Needed to Make Alex's Armor

Piece of Armor	Number of Diamonds
TOTAL	

THE ENDERMAN

Read about Endermen. Then define the bolded words on the next page.
Hint: The answers are in the story.

An Enderman is tall and skinny with long arms. It is black and has creepy pink eyes. An Enderman is not dangerous but it does like to cause mischief (trouble). It takes blocks that players have put down and moves them to other places. It can also teleport, which means it can move itself in an instant. Enderman will spawn—or multiply—in darkness. It is harmed by water. Never stare at an Enderman because it will turn hostile, or mean.

Word	Meaning
Mischief	....
Teleport	....
Spawn	....
Hostile	....

Bonus: How did the story give you clues to what the words mean?

....

WHAT ARE IGLOOS?

Read about igloos.
Then answer the questions on the next page.

Igloos make a great pit stop if you are traveling.
You will find them in cold, snowy biomes—like
the Ice Plains and Cold Taiga. If you get cold or
hungry, you should find an empty igloo. Inside
will be a cozy room with everything you need.
It will have a rug, a crafting table, a torch, and a
heater. It will have lots of food stored on a shelf.
You will also find blankets and warm clothes.
Just watch out for polar bears!

What is the main idea of this text?

A) Igloos have blankets and clothes inside.

B) Igloos make a great pit stop for travelers.

C) Igloos can be found in cold, snowy biomes.

D) You should never go inside an igloo.

List three reasons why a player may want to go inside an igloo.

1.

2.

3.

THE CAT IN THE JUNGLE

Read the story about the cat in the jungle.
Then answer the questions on the next page.

Will gazed at the trees stretching toward the sky. They were getting taller now. Thicker, too, and covered with lush green vines. I made it! thought Will. A shiver of excitement ran down his spine.

"Stop!" Mina suddenly whispered.

Will whirled around, expecting to come face to face with a monster. Instead, Mina was pointing at . . .

"A cat?" asked Will. He could barely see the spotted cat prowling in the thicket of trees.

"Not yet," Mina whispered. "He's an ocelot now—a wild cat. But if I feed him a little fish, I might be able to tame him."

"You have fish?" asked Will. His mouth watered at the thought.

From Lost in the Jungle: Secrets of an Overworld Survivor by Greyson Mann, Sky Pony Press, 2017.

What clues tell you that Will and Mina are walking deeper into a jungle?

How does Will feel about the jungle?

Which character seems to know more about the jungle? Use proof from the story.

How can you tell that Will is hungry?

ANSWER KEY

PAGE 2

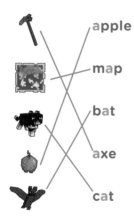

apple

map

bat

axe

cat

PAGE 3

1. apple
2. bat
3. map
4. cat
5. axe

PAGE 4

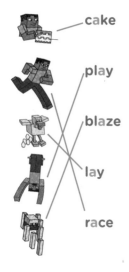

cake

play

blaze

lay

race

PAGE 5

1. cake
2. blaze
3. race
4. lay
5. play

PAGE 6

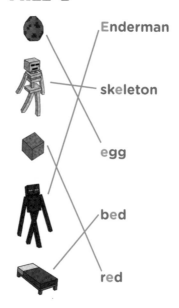

Enderman

skeleton

egg

bed

red

PAGE 7

1. egg
2. red
3. skeleton
4. bed
5. Enderman

PAGE 8

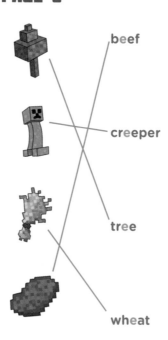

beef

creeper

tree

wheat

she

PAGE 9

1. wheat
2. beef
3. creeper
4. tree
5. she

PAGE 10

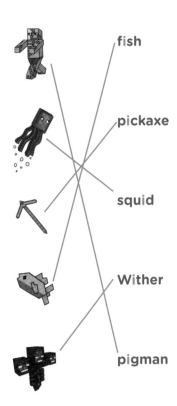

fish

pickaxe

squid

Wither

pigman

PAGE 11

1. pigman
2. pickaxe
3. squid
4. Wither
5. fish

PAGE 12

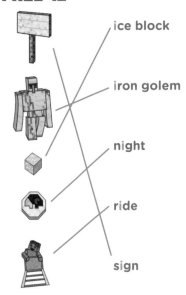

ice block

iron golem

night

ride

sign

PAGE 13

1. ice blocks
2. iron golem
3. sign
4. night
5. ride

PAGE 14

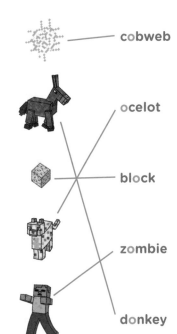

cobweb

ocelot

block

zombie

donkey

PAGE 15

6. ocelot
7. blocks
8. zombie
9. cobwebs
10. donkey

PAGE 16

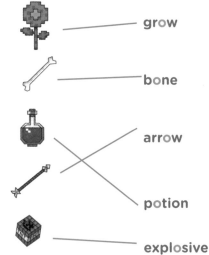

grow

bone

arrow

potion

explosive

PAGE 17

1. grow
2. bone
3. potion
4. arrow
5. explosive

PAGE 18

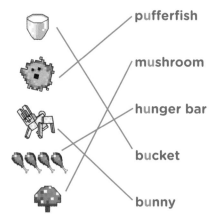

pufferfish

mushroom

hunger bar

bucket

bunny

PAGE 19

1. bunny
2. bucket
3. hunger bar
4. pufferfish
5. mushrooms

PAGE 20

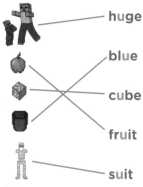

huge

blue

cube

fruit

suit

PAGE 21

1. blue
2. cube   4. fruit
3. suit   5. huge

PAGES 22-23

1. The green creepers dance.

2. The player crafts an iron sword.

3. Alex fills the open chest.

4. The baby zombie rides a chicken.

5. The skeleton shoots a sharp arrow.

PAGE 24-25

Pigs spawn on sandstone.	False
Pigs live in the Overworld.	True
Pigs like water.	False
A piglet is an adult pig.	False
It takes twenty minutes for piglets to grow into pigs.	True

PAGES 26-27

The wolf's fur is ...   black eyes
A wild wolf has ....   a red collar
A mean wolf has ....   gray
A tame wolf has ....   red eyes

PAGES 28-29

What color are the cow's spots?
The cow's spots are **gray**.
How do cows walk?
Cows walk **slowly**.
What does a cow follow?
A cow follows **wheat**.

PAGES 28–29 (CONTINUED)

What do you need to milk a cow?
You need a **bucket** to milk a cow.

PAGES 30–31

The horse comes in **seven** colors.
The horse likes eating carrots because they are **crunchy**.
A **saddle** lets you ride the horse.
When a horse is tame, it shows **hearts**.

PAGES 32–33

Zombies are
❑ Fast ☒ Slow ❑ Quiet

What kind of sounds do zombies make?
❑ Moaning ❑ Screaming ☒ Groaning

What can kill a zombie?
☒ Sunlight ❑ Darkness ❑ Other zombies

Who can a zombie call for help?
❑ Wolves ☒ Other zombies ❑ Dragons

If a zombie attacks you, it can turn you into a
❑ Robot ☒ Zombie ❑ Zombie robot

PAGES 34–35

Creepers can sneak up on you because they are **very quiet**.
Creepers might be hiding in a **cave**.
If they explode, you could be **harmed**.
Creepers have a fear of **cats**.
Creepers can't open doors, but they can climb **ladders**.

PAGES 36–37

The Ender dragon is a **boss mob**.
The dragon lives in **the End**.
The dragon flies in **circles** in the sky.
The balls of fire are **purple**.
To get an egg from an Ender Dragon, you have to **destroy** it.

PAGES 38–39

What is the main idea of this story?
The boats in the new version of Minecraft are better than the boats in the old version.

Give three details to support the main idea:
Note: answer may vary, but should include 3 of the 4 details below
1. *The new boats are stronger and don't break apart so easily.*
2. *The new boats come with paddles.*
3. *The new boats go faster than the old boats.*
4. *The new boats can carry more people.*

PAGES 40–41

The ghast:
B. Floated
The ghast was:
C. Sad
The ghast's mouth and eyes are:
B. Black
The ghast shot:
A. Fireballs
The arrow almost hit the ghast's:
C. Legs

PAGES 42–43

Potion Colors and Their Effects

COLOR	EFFECT
Green	Jump high
Blue	See at night
Purple	Restore health
Red	Strength
Yellow	Health boost
Orange	Fire protection

PAGES 44–45

What is the cause of the mother's anger?
Steve ate all of his birthday cake after she told him not to eat any of it.
What is the effect of the mother's anger?
Steve has to call his friends to tell them his birthday party is cancelled.

PAGES 46–47

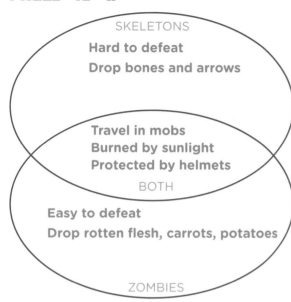

SKELETONS
Hard to defeat
Drop bones and arrows

BOTH
Travel in mobs
Burned by sunlight
Protected by helmets

ZOMBIES
Easy to defeat
Drop rotten flesh, carrots, potatoes

PAGES 48–49

2   Steve clears a flat spot for his garden.
3   Steve collects seeds.
5   Steve digs a hole for water.
1   Steve makes a hoe.
6   Steve puts a torch next to his crops.
4   Steve plants the seeds.

PAGES 50–51

Piece of Armor	Number of Diamonds
Helmet	5
Chestplate	8
Leggings	7
Boots	4
TOTAL	24

PAGES 52–53

Word	Meaning
Mischief	Trouble
Teleport	Move in an instant
Spawn	Multiply
Hostile	Mean

PAGES 52–53 (CONTINUED)

Bonus: The different ways definitions are given are by
 1) using the definition in parentheses (trouble),
2) using the phrase "which means" after the word and before the definition,
3) using dashes—such as these—to explain the definition, and
4) using a comma and the word "or" before the definition.

PAGES 54–55

What is the main idea of this text?
B) Igloos make a great pit stop for travelers.

Note: Answers may vary. This is a sample of possible answers.
List three reasons why a player may want to go inside an igloo.
1. Igloos have everything you need.
2. Igloos have food stored on shelves.
3. Igloos have blankets and warm clothes.

PAGES 56–57

What clues show that Will and Mina are deeper into the jungle?
The clues are that the trees were getting taller, thicker, and covered with lush green vines.

How does Will feel about the jungle?
Excited and/or nervous.

Which character seems to know more about the jungle? Use proof from the story?
Mina seems to know more because she isn't as nervous and she knows that the ocelot is not a cat.

How can you tell that Will is hungry?
His mouth waters at the thought of fish.